birra-bina-birra yaryanbuwaliya yandu

gentle whispers from the every'when

I first encountered Uncle Glenn Loughrey's compelling poems, and the yarns that inform them, in our new 'Blak n Blues' collaboration: an intercultural conversation in Blues music and poetry.

Coming from the Indigenous perspective, his observations are both refreshingly personal and universal, creating an engaging space to consider deeply important issues. I've personally found listening to this wonderful work fascinating and enriching. Speak the poems out loud!

Fiona Boyes
Award-winning blues and roots guitarist
Songwriter and vocalist

This collection is an invitation to another way of being. It is an offering, a guide and a gift. There is reflection, beauty and truth here alongside the reminder that we are all custodians of the land.

Covering the many experiences of cultural dispossession and yearning for a wholeness of self and of society, these poems – with their clear, direct voice – shoot arrows of meaning straight to the reader's heart. They ask how to be in the world, point to the wound caused by separation from Country and the healing made possible by returning.

Katharine Downey
The Leaf Bookshop
Melbourne

Glenn Loughrey, Aboriginal elder, Anglican priest, activist, artist and poet has produced a book of poems and reflections gathered on his journey through life. They reflect his experiences growing up in Australia since the 1950s. He shares not just stories and experiences but the cultural knowledge and wisdom that shapes his perception, sensibility and his very being.

Topics touched upon include mothers, fathers, country, life, language, belonging, hurt, connection, the Voice, spirituality and ecology. Somehow, through this writing, this wisdom, accumulated over tens of thousands of years, connects and seeps into the reader's awareness. Highly recommended.

Prof. Michael McGartland
Clinical and Counselling Psychologist
St Kilda

birra-bina-birra yaryanbuwaliya yandu

gentle whispers from the every'when

glenn loughrey

Published in Australia by
Coventry Press
33 Scoresby Road
Bayswater VIC 3153

ISBN 9781922589668

Copyright © Glenn Loughrey 2025

All rights reserved. Other than for the purposes and subject to the conditions prescribed under the *Copyright Act*, no part of this publication may be reproduced, stored in a retrieval system, or transmitted in any form or by any means, electronic, mechanical, photocopying, recording or otherwise, without the prior permission of the publisher.

Scripture quotations are from the *New Revised Standard Version Bible*, copyright 1989, Division of Christian Education of the National Council of the Churches of Christ in the United States of America. Used by permission. All rights reserved.

Catalogue-in-Publication entry is available from the National Library of Australia
http://catalogue.nla.gov.au

Cover design by Ian James – www.jgd.com.au
Text design by Coventry Press
Set in EB Garamond

Printed in Australia

table of contents

About Language ix
introduction xi
   mothers repose 1
   gugaa 3
   maliyan 4
   girray burrawarra 5
   yanhana garray 6
   gulaman biran 7
   the drip (the dripping wall) 9
   if jesus was born aboriginal 11
   ngiyanggarang - the voice 13
   murrambang 15
   wiradjuri-dhu 17
   wiradjuri 19
   nguram-bang-wirray - placeless 21
   ngahdhu wiray 25
   ya-l-ali-ga-rra wirray 28
   burral 30
   bimbarra buguwiny yindang 32
   yuyang 35
   exile I 37
   wrong shoes 39
   exile II 40
   known 41
   where were you 43
   another australian soldier dies in afghanistan 45
   the roustabouts clout 47
   song for a childhood lost 49
   ya gotta limp a little 51
   lost somewhere in between 53

i wasnt done walking	55
bulbil - feather	57
bila ngayirr	58
circles	59
yes in a world of no	61
you are like dogs	71

About Language

Aboriginal language is not English; and it is not English using Aboriginal words.
Each Aboriginal Australian Language Group that stems from Pama Nyungan (95% of all Aboriginal language groups) has its own unique language words to describe the purpose of a particular place.

Language is not just about the written word and how it is put together. Language is also about how a people think – their world view and the idealistic goals they live by.

Think about how you would transfer information today if you did not know how to write and had to be just verbal? It takes the use of different skills and abilities. Not less than those who write, just different and, I would argue, much more creative.

Durru-ga-rra Mayinybang Gunhi (doo roo garra Mine bung gore knee): 'What country do you belong to?' in Wiradjuri? A powerful question that becomes even more potent when you know Gunhi means mother.

Wiradjuri are Maternal, law-based people. Everything comes from our mother. Every part of our identity is connected back to the identity of our Gunhi.

The brilliance and adaptability of oral cultures to create and embed an entire health, governance, ceremonial, education, economic and ecological system without one single written word is mind blowing and should be lauded as a feat worthy of much respect and focus to be restored, used and understood by all Australians.

In Aboriginal language, most if not all the meanings of the words in the sentences are built into the words themselves. As a result, the order in which the words are used is a matter of choice, linked to what is the most important thing at the moment to the speaker. Aboriginal language tends to link ideas in a Kinship network because they connect ideas according to how they are related to each other.

Language is about people, their lives, how they relate to one another and how they live together in their systems universe.

When you think of Aboriginal people's language – even when we speak English, we say and write "we" when talking about ourselves and the Colonial Heritage and European speakers say "I". This simple difference identifies how we think and feel within our societies and systems. What we reveal is our core subconscious motivation – how we see the world. Our inside identity never changes. Putting my extended Kinship First so I can be happy and content from the Aboriginal Australian people; and putting myself First so my family can be happy and content from the Australia people.

Nola Turner-Jensen

Nola is a Wiradyuri women who is an Aboriginal Spoken Navigation researcher from the Balbu clan group of West Galari NSW.

She is currently a Candidate with the Indigenous Knowledge Institute at the University of Melbourne, undertaking a Doctorate of Indigenous Philosophy and in her final year of a Diversity and Inclusion Fellowship with Melbourne Science Faculty, researching Sound Codes that identify sacred Aboriginal sites.

She is also Co-Chair of the West Galari Wiradyuri Traditional Owner Corporation and is a multiple published author.

introduction

writing in an aboriginal manner is interesting for someone raised in the western language the following is a selection of words ideas thoughts without punctuation such as full stops commas capitals language depends on place people circumstances all influencing how its heard and in this case read remembering that our language was spoken acted sung danced painted but not written down this process of writing in language adds another layer of complexity to an already complex system of communication

speaker and hearer engage in a process situated in the circumstances they find themselves they speak out of that in deference and respect of each other and their kinship relationships amongst other factors that impact all conversations sentences are not sentences in the sense that english depicts them they are a collection of words prefixes suffixes and relationships that when translated sound like what english speakers are used to that may not necessarily be the case and it requires nuancing to understand meaning

words are often multifunctional that is the same word carries different meanings in different circumstances and within the various dialects of language groups translating english words and their accompanying concepts into wiradjuri takes some work to discern just how to speak those concepts into a language without similar philosophical underpinnings and concepts

words in language are kinship based all of life is kinship based each word is related directly to the words around it in order to elicit meaning and communication no word stands alone without context and kinship reading wiradjuri requires an understanding of the kinship relationship of the words used the people who wrote or spoke and those reading or listening to it and the context in which the transaction or relationship takes place it is not as it looks you will hear and read differently depending on factors that influence your engagement

i am not a linguist nor a proficient speaker of wiradjuri i am a learner and this process of writing and transferring meaning into language is how i learn i teach myself or perhaps more correctly the language teaches me not everything here is in language yet some may never be others will be as i progress in my journey and gain proficiency

in reading the following allow the cadence and rhythm of the words speak resist the urge to add your own punctuation to make it make sense read it in the tradition of wiradjuri language allowing it to adapt and reimagine itself in your speaking of what is written as i am typing this the spell check keeps adding punctuation such as capitals just because that's what we do in English (just did it again)

note i suggest you speak it out not just read passively a language or a way of writing that is predicated on an oral tradition that only gains its true voice when spoken unconsciously and without the need to perform it when we read silently we can find ourselves interpreting the script when reading out loud we are allowing the script to be its own performance in that we hear see and experience something new hidden in the words spaces places and moments when we encounter them

finally a note on the purpose of this publication while there are moments this book touches on the christian myth it does so not to validate that myth but to interrogate it from a first peoples perspective it does so because of the role christianity has played in the colonial project and the assumption that australian values and way of life is based on the christian values and philosophies this document questions that and challenges those who believe so to consider another perspective the perspective that is embedded is a very different way of being and seeing the world the poems range from a direct focus on the myths sitting at the heart of the australian

introduction

story to a nuanced and oblique gaze at what we tell ourselves about ourselves

first peoples spirituality and being has been here for some 65000 years some 57000 years before the abrahamic religions it has developed on a kinship basis the relationship between all things and not on a personal interaction with the divine or spirit christianity as one of the abrahamic myths has only in the last 500 years become the universal spirituality of coloniality and modernity and through the patronage of colonisation become imposed on ancient people

the question this raises is does this entitle it the right to replace what was here before or even to interrogate the ancient and appropriate it for its own use i would suggest no i would suggest that we need to read christianity for example through the gaze of first peoples spirituality and judge it against what was here before this makes this book a decolonial project delinking from the universal western european patriarchal paternalistic overlay of privilege and reexisting the ancient which was here before and remains today

personally this book reflects my own journey into and away from traditional religion and belief taught as the basis of our present existence back to what is embedded within and remains embedded in country and kin i am at this moment moving further and further away from the traditional christian paradigm and may one day disappear into my past a past that has always existed by its absence as an uninhabited void within my soul

glenn loughrey

mothers repose

earth sleeks out
under trees on tiptoes
toward the wandering waters
still billabongs
choruses of crows
yawning gorges
gaping gaps between
the vibrancy of green
brown and red
its forever colours
seasons announcing their arrival
in the running of eels
the burrowing wombat
the swarming bogong
kangaroos birthing
the signs of the season to come
dry riverbeds
flooding plains
burning scrub

mothers repose
our sure foundation
of waiting and being
identity and belonging
deep beyond deep
encircling our standing
walking resting sitting
breathing and non-breathing
stillness
silence
no thing
yet
moving

speaking
everything

earth
my mother
my country

we are home when on country when at home we remember that we are the child of the earth that both is and holds country each step we take each breath we breathe and feel is courtesy of our mother this planet and in particular this patch of country which is us we are one with country our mother country remains regardless of us and what we do but we are asked to care for her aware that we live in a dependent relationship with her and all she holds this is no mystery nor is it defined by science and intellectual knowledge it just is we are not detached from her and she from us she is the one who gives life without limits mother relies on our connection to her to remain alive and free to give life to all she wishes to mothers have a way of being that gives a sense of security and safety even when threatened or under pressure a mothers repose

gugaa[1]

    ancient beast
    of the sandy plains
    kurrajong trees
    meandering creeks
    flicking forked tongue
    tasting the air
    sensing presence
    absence
    beauty
    danger
    lumbering purposefully
    rising to a challenge
    slipping away
    when opportunity invites
    watching from the treetops
    tea tree bushes
    granite rocks
    lazing in the sun
    beast of this soil
    kin of creation
    totem of our people

wiradjuri are the people of the no – wirray we have the no the ability to say no not now not here not that way we are also the people of gugaa ubiquitous ever present ancient gabaas would say prehistoric we would say from the dreaming the beginning of time i learnt early on how special they were we never killed them unless there was no other way to handle a chicken pilfering ancestor i remember as a young child catching a large gugaa in a rabbit trap it was angry as i wasnt allowed to kill it i had to find a way to release it and let it go it took some ingenuity and a great deal of courage to do so but he ran away free

---

1 goanna – wiradjuri totem

maliyan[2]

>that fella up there
>thermally circling
>just below the stars
>surveying
>plains and valleys
>desert and forest
>rivers and billabongs
>the wanderings of creatures
>great and small
>i
>others
>always watching
>always there
>
>maliyan

that fella up there i learn him he watches all i do that fella he flies around watches all on the ground and in the air he is the wedge tail eagle and he knows all he will tell me when i am ready to learn more but i learn from him wisdom comes from country from all that makes up country and if you walk slowly without rushing, with respect – yindyamarra – you will learn from all that shares place and space with you

---

2 thanks to uncle waddy

girray burrawarra[3]
   – dont make dust

burrawarra bunan	dust rises up
muglinya[4] giyin	eyes itch
dhawurra[5] girarumarra	wind blows
garra[6]	stop
winhuminya[7]	sit down
winhangarra[8]	listen
windimanha[9]	wait
yany-ndhu gulbara[10]	so you understand

being in a hurry is not our way we wait we do not hurry we do not make dust if something is worth doing it is worth doing in the time it takes to do it no short cuts no rush no place to be

as a child i used to help muster sheep dad would wait at the gate to count them through he would watch how we moved the sheep and used the dog more than once he asked do you have somewhere else to be i answered no each time he would reply think you do you raised dust it was not his way it is not our way we know how to wait

---

3 dust
4 eyes
5 wind
6 stop
7 sit down
8 listen
9 wait
10 so you understand?

yanhana garray[11]
– walk country

yanhana garray[12]	*walk country*
yindyamarra[13]	*slowly*
winhangarra[14]	*listen*
mambuwalabu ngaanhabu gulbalabul[15]	*look and see*
winhangadurinya[16]	*reflect*
murungiyalinya[17]	*revive*
yany-ndhu gulbara[18]	*so you understand*

the relationship with country is the primary relationship it is the one that explains the meaning of life and ensures life continues walking country is not about going somewhere it is a conversation with all around you a conversation that engages all your senses in order for you to understand what is happening and how you are to respond

my father would say walk your country listen carefully and you will hear what it has to say and what it wants you to do he walked his country on the farm everyday

---

11 walk country
12 walk country
13 slowly
14 listen
15 look and see
16 reflect
17 revive
18 so you understand?

gulaman biran[19]

gulaman biran	coolaman boy
wir-marra	touch the wind
balabaia-ya-li-nya[20]	whisper
nguram-bang bala-dhu[21]	i am country
bangal-buwu-rayi bala-dhu[22]	i am indigenous of the universe
nganhi-wal bala-dhu[23]	i am up there
nhanha-dhar bala-dhu[24]	i am here
nganhi-dhar bala-dhu[25]	i am deep down
ngiyawagunhaanha bala-dhu[26]	i am always here
baran-dhi balan-dha bala-dhu[27]	i was here from the beginning
yandhul[28]	i am here now
ngumhuwi-nguwur[29]	i am beyond all
gulaman biran bala-dhu	i am coolaman boy
yany-ndhu gulbara	so you understand

we always exist we are here forever for there is no beginning and no end just this moment we carry country and the universe within us

---

19 coolaman boy
20 whisper
21 home country
22 country as all the world
23 up there (distant in space and time)
24 down here
25 down there (distance in space and time.)
26 always be
27 in the beginning long ago first
28 now
29 beyond on the other side

we are not separate from but integral to all that is there are parallels here with the christian myth of jesus as told in the gospel of johns first chapter on which this poem is based translating this and other key christian texts nuances the meaning deepens its power and widens its relevance it is more than the universal flatness of english can express

the drip (the dripping wall)

i fall here
dripping down the sandstone
weaving time
between the rocks
under the foliage
reaching out precariously
settling in the moss
on my journey
to the clear pools below
where mothers come
babies are born and
life begins again
in this harsh land

i fall here
as i have done
from the beginning of time
continuing today
into the long forever
in the worst drought
devastating bushfire or
raging flood
i drip without ceasing
revealing the possibility of life
hope in the first breath
wonder of birth
gift of
water and blood
alpha and omega

yany-ndhu gulbara

on the banks of the goulburn river there is a sandstone wall that
never runs dry it drips constantly into the pools below these pools were

10   birra-bina-birra...

places women came to give birth it is a sacred space which played a central role in the brett whitely incident of the early 1970s when he painted fake aboriginal art on the banks of the river while naked he was pursued by locals lead by my father intent on shooting him for desecrating the site it was not his paintings that mattered but the fact he was naked in a sacred womens space

if jesus was born aboriginal

if jesus was born aboriginal
he would be
born under tree
in the arms of his two mothers
rising out of his mother country
bringing with him from her
the knowledge and wisdom of
the ancestors of his other mother mary
and his father the great creator being

if jesus was born aboriginal
he would be
surrounded by all his cousins
kookaburra and crow
kangaroo and wallaby
goanna and snake
gum tree and acacia
wattle and blackbutt
baaka and martuwarra[30]

if jesus was born aboriginal
he would be
lain on the ground
to bond with his mother country
to live out his vocation of
custodial care for all
being responsible to and for
all who live alongside him
respecting life itself in all things

if Jesus was born aboriginal
he would

---

30 baaka or darling river; martuwarra or fitzroy river

learn to be at home
with country family and kin
growing in wisdom and knowledge
an elder sharing knowledge and wisdom
guiding and leading
respecting and caring
for all who share his home with him

....

what if jesus was not born in palestine what if jesus was born here on country what would he have been like how would he have lived and who would he have been seeking freedom from for his people

one could argue that the birth of jesus is a foundational myth of colonial australia some would say the foundational myth yet it is a story from another time and place it was not founded as a universal story but one that spoke directly to the needs of a group of people in an occupied space who understood themselves as gods chosen ones

does this colonial story resonate with indigenous australia is it relevant and if it does in some way what would that look like through the eyes of the many different language groups experiences would those who colonized and remain the dominant culture be seen in this reimagining as the occupying forces and the church in all its forms the religious leaders who spoke against the freedom jesus offered

just asking

ngiyanggarang - the voice

– (at christmas we "celebrate the institution of the voice in the divine constitution of the universe"[31] john 1)

>
> jesus is god spoken
> on country
> from country
> honouring the country of
> his father and his mother
> speaking truth into each
> from the other
>
> jesus the christ
> is god's voice
> into the realm of humanity
> and
> humanity's voice
> into the realm of god
>
> jesus the christ
> is the sovereignty of God
> incarnate
> walking
> with the sovereign people
> of god's creation
>
> the incarnated christ
> becomes the voice of
> god's creation
> at the throne of god
> interceding on our behalf

---

[31] gwl sermon 25122022

sovereignty remains
honoured in both places
in both realms
each speaking truth to that other
responding
to bring wholeness
fulfilment
cleansing to all

yany-ndhu gulbara

christian sovereignty is unlike the hard external sovereignty of governments built on rules laws books words power it is more like indigenous sovereignty which is relational for us sovereignty is bound by the relationship we have with country and all that we share it with it is not imposed or enforced it has no beginning nor end there are no boundaries sovereignty is a gift the grows and becomes as one lives in relationship with country it is this relational focus that we share with christianity it is why our country needs indigenous sovereignty in the constitution to complete the circle and make us as a country whole.

murrambang
– justice

    justice
    wholeness
    belonging place
    custodial being
    respect
    responsibility
    reciprocity
    putting back
    bringing in

    not revenge
    payback
    brutality
    disrespecting place
    and ancestors tradition
    held in country
    becoming the invader
    acting cruelty
    separation
    disconnection

    justice
    seeks repair
    honours country
    and all it holds
    the wisdom of the ancients
    the experience of the elders
    the life of the people
    and the every'when

    yany-ndhu gulbara

much of what we talk about today has to do with reconciliation without justice it is about inclusion of first nations people in the dominant society and a commitment to be nice to each other without the hard work necessary it does not speak of what needs to be done structurally in order that we meet as equals or as paul kelly writes meet me in the middle of the air the statement from the heart is not about making all people one and free or in our context all people white and free the voice and the statement are about redeeming us all from the original sin of invasion and genocide it is the decolonial option in an australian setting where we delink from the colonial imperative and re-exist the memory what was here bcp before cook and phillip

wiradjuri-dhu
– sovereignty never ceded

>body carries body
>body is country
>country carries country
>we are place
>never removed
>always there
>here
>everywhere
>everywhen
>
>sovereignty
>belongs in place
>country
>body
>never ceded
>breathing this space
>this body
>this place
>creation
>people
>you
>me
>
>*yany-ndhu gulbara*

sovereignty is relational it is held in relationship with country country is not simply the dirt under our feet but sky country the various countries below us all that live in these spaces and whom we share it with human and non-human sovereignty is how we live with a custodial ethic with all of this

it is not a legal title in the sense of the western private state ownership model it is a binding to all in order to maintain wholeness and wellbeing for all there is no i in mob sovereignty comes embedded *in our body no one can give it up no one can take it it is my body my country you may deny me my rights but you can never take my sovereignty*

wiradjuri

– language and country are inseparable that is language is country and country is language in this case wiradjuri and its dialects is both language and country

wiradjuri spoken
tradition
transmitted

wiradjuri lived
tradition
incarnated

wiradjuri unknown
tradition
untold

wiradjuri unheard
tradition
embedded
at birth
country within
speaking its own language
in the absence
of words

yany-ndhu gulbara

language is a part of our dna speaking language connects you to country seasons time space context nuance without language it is difficult to be yourself part of the rationale of coloniality is the erasure of all that makes you human language is a key identifier which is erased almost immediately being made to speak anothers language means you have to think like them raising young people without their language makes it harder for them to maintain their aboriginality that which determines how they think feel become

yet language is not an added extra it is embedded in the body even if not spoken out loud the language of country whispers within rising when needed not as words or sounds but as feelings emotions sensing walking country whinangarra listening hearing reflecting gives you the capacity to recognise language in the unspoken in the absence of words

nguram-bang-wirray - placeless

placeless
is not just
having no place
you call home

it is having
no place
calling you home

no place
knowing you
as belonging

belonging
on in with
all in place

alone
lonely
unmissed

not heard
seen
or felt

by those
on in with
place

untethered
uncentred
ungrounded

free
yet
not free

freedom
comes from
place

place
allows you
to be

place
bestows freedom
to move

become
belong
move away

move back
and away
and back again

without
fear of
getting lost

being lost
unfound
unplaced

placeless
is place
without our country

our mother
songline
dreaming

kin
dirt beneath
our feet

in our veins
body
spirit

it is
being empty
of all meaning

purpose
hope
possibility

of the promises of
every'when
every'where for ever

it leaves us
listless
hopeless

frustrated
angry
self-destructive

cartoon stereotypes
others name
and we inhabit

we are
in search of place
home

going home
without a map
yet going

for in going
we find what
we are looking for

dimly
uncertainly
hesitatingly

home will
be revealed
when there

yany-ndhu gulbara

country is our identifier place holds us to our custodial vocation our innate wisdom and pedagogy without place we are no thing real dispossession uproots us disconnects us from the layers and layers of tradition wisdom spirituality and language embedded beneath our feet above our head and in the space around us

when we are exiled from country we cannot carry on our conversation with it despite it being a part of our dna distance separates stops the flow of knowledge and tradition which we need to be truly who we are it is why we wither and die from the inside out if we remain placeless for too long going home getting back on country is necessary to revitalise our spirit and close the circle of wellness and healing

ngahdhu wiray
– not i

>who i am
>is not mine
>to declare
>
>others define
>who what
>i am
>
>my story
>is interpreted
>mediated
>
>through the
>language of
>the other
>
>the one
>with the power
>to designate
>
>life
>hope
>possibility
>
>or stereotypes
>fitting
>story
>
>their meaning
>making
>myth
>
>i am not i
>i am who you
>want to make me

since invasion
that is
how it is

nothing has changed

yany-ndhu gulbara

written after reading meg foster's interpretation of jimmy governor in her book "boundary crossers"

the story of governor has been appropriated by keneally and schepsi in the 1970s, by reynolds around the same time and now foster, each over laying an identity that does not allow for his voice to be heard

he wasn't a fighter for rights or a bush ranger he was a man who snapped under the colonial pressure of shame

his 'rampage' may have begun in an emotional outburst but the subsequent murders he committed were not he had a long list of people who had wronged him, and he went methodically about the process of pay-back these were people he knew drank with played cricket with and worked for cutting fenceposts among other tasks people he at one time or another saw as friends

the list of victims would have been larger if such as the davis men at ulan and the piper boys at uarbry where at home when he called he met others such as the auld boys (postmen) whom he acknowledged as he rode past their camp outside coolah he camped just a little way up the road from them he had gone to school with them and often camped with them when they met on the road he rode past the loughrey house at loughville and waved to those inside as he went to water his horses at the creek in both cases the aulds and the loughreys did not know about the crimes he had committed in the loughrey's case the murder of herb mackay a couple miles back toward the gulgong road

while he adapted to his situation to write letters about rights and acclaim himself as a bushranger these were not his initial motivations there was another governor who is rightfully called the *last aboriginal bushranger and that was roy jimmy's brother or perhaps as some letter writers to the papers of the time suggested jimmy's son*

we do a disservice to him and many who have had to live with the colonial pressure of shame by simply pigeonholing him them in a convenient category such as bushranger and other categories of deficit for our own purposes it is much more complicated and we owe it to them to engage with the complexity in such a way that we respect the humanity of each despite their actions

i lived a parallel story to this one and perhaps i will write more on it later it could have been as devastating as this story if those involved had encountered one another it is a personal story and i am working my way through it to respect those involved and those still living who are connected to it

the governor story is bigger than the purposes we give it and has reverberated through the experience of all who live in the shadow of colonial shame

ya-l-ali-ga-rra wirray
– don't do it again don't repeat what you did before

    promises
are made
to be broken
at least promises
made to blakfellas by gabaas
there have been
so may promises

ya-l-ali-ga-rra wirray

some in law
some in agreements
some in dirt
placed in anothers
hand
some spoken at places
redfern
gama
parliament house
and more
many more

ya-l-ali-ga-rra wirray

some have names
mabo
stolen generation
nter[32]

---

[32] northern territory emergency response

some by gabaas
some by gabaas and mob
none have
it could be argued
done what they promised

ya-l-ali-ga-rra wirray

we are still
placeless
deficit
unheard and
unseen

ya-l-ali-ga-rra wirray

will the woodford statement
be different

ya-l-ali-ga-rra wirray

yany-ndhu gulbara

first peoples are the people of promises promises made by those who came later promises of inclusion privilege possibility these promises are made by prime ministers ministers governments institutions corporates and the general public rarely do any survive past the opportunistic memory of those who made them we accept them because we are always hopeful that one time sometime these promises will be real and will bring about real change in our world they disappear from sight so quickly there is barely a trace of their existence

the promise to enshrine our voice in the constitution to recognise us is the acceptance of our invitation and appears to be one of goodwill be careful not allow this promise to go the way of the others if it does the implications for our people may die this may be the last promise broken

burral

– place or soil upon which a child is born and where the placenta is buried

>it is here
>on this country
>under this tree
>in this place
>a child was born
>
>it is here
>in this country
>of birth
>the gift of a mother
>lies
>
>cradled
>in the mother of all
>is the one blood
>we all share
>as kin and kind
>
>it is here
>tradition and lore
>story and song
>now embedded
>is returned home
>
>it is here
>we remember
>we own no thing
>what we come with
>is but a gift to be returned

it is here
we place in country
our body our country
adding to the richness
out of which we were born

yany-ndhu gulbara

life is a circle we rise from our mother country and return to it closing the circle and making our offering for the future lives which will follow this aboriginal vocation each of us have two mothers the mother who gives us birth and the other gives life for us and all it is this maternal relationship which empowers our being and makes us real we honour and respect both it is through our mothers we find our cultural language spirituality it begins with both our mothers and continues until we return to the one who gave and takes our life as a gift for another

bimbarra buguwiny yindang
– the slow burn

    slow burn
    honouring country
    small
    timely
    cool
    i remember
    windless nguruban
    in bangalang
    when the undergrowth
    was still dry enough
    to burn
    without fury
    creeping
    underneath branches
    over rocks
    friendly and warm
    embracing life
    tickling the belly of country
    calling forth energy
    hidden within

    i remember
    watching from the edges
    as flames danced
    to and fro
    under a deep black
    star filled night sky
    twinkling in time
    with the burning below
    now and then
    i used the tree branch

i held in my hand
to discourage a wayward
flame or ember
from escaping
into mischief

i remember
the stillness
grounding me
so i stood still
aware and alert
but unmoving and
free to be
one with the cleansing
of country
a custodial act of
responsibility
reciprocity
respect

i remember
the smoke
as it wafted around
garraba-dhi (my body)
remnants of
dhumba (spotted gums)
dalawang (apple boxes)
burrin (mountain oak)
darri (old stumps of grass)
crackling in the moonlight
welcoming me
on to their country
with the annual
smoking ceremony

i remember
walking away
going home
yura-ba-rra (sleeping) maintaining the integrity of the fire as it
burnt in on itself
senses alive with
yirayin (light)
balgal (sound, noise)
yuwar (smell, aroma)
of another evening
on the slow burn

yany-ndhu gulbara

it was a ritual we would gather early just my father my brother and me we would go to the selected hilly spot where the undergrowth was thickest and stand still my father would feel the breeze sense the moisture in the autumn sky and discern the burn we would find ourselves a branch with a thick covering of green leaves and take our designated spaces at the edge my father would then carefully burn a figure 8 where he had chosen to burn our task was to watch the edges maintaining the integrity of the fire as it burnt in on itself this was not a wholesale burn just in those spaces that needed it and which had not been burnt for a couple of years

yuyang
– redtail black cockatoo

    yuyang
    glossy
    black
    raucous
    its tail
    embellished with fiery
    red feathers

    yuyang
    rarely seen alone
    no one notices
    a solitary bird
    silent
    black and lonely
    against the sky
    red feathers furled

    yuyang
    in company
    black
    loud and proud
    of the now
    unfurled red feathers
    everyone notices
    if they notice such things
    flying west to east
    heralds rain
    when
    count the formation
    to divine its arrival

    yany-ndhu gulbara

my father watched the elements for signs of rain and weather he was a long range weather forecaster and watched the stars for information he was rarely wrong in the midrange he watched the behaviour of animals such as the kangaroo whose breeding habits signified what the season would or would not be for the immediate future the flight of the black cockatoo and the movement of ants were all signs used to predicate with accuracy the weather on the way the number of black cockatoos flying west to east would indicate when the rains would come and how much it would be

exile I

once
he had a dream
a few acres of their own
a place to farm
to use his skills and wisdom
make a future for his boys

a place in society for her
she deserved that

it was not much
but it had potential
they had to see that
he had a plan
he knew it would work
or he was the best farmer
in the district

he wore his sunday best
so did she

off they went to the bank
full of hope and ....

they said no

he knew why

and he felt the shame

so did she

and the boys

he went and got drunk

> what else can you do
> in exile?[33]

not long after the 1967 referendum success my father and mother had a dream the farm up the road was for sale along with the post office franchise they put together a rough business plan and went to the bank we went with them dressed in our sunday best while we sat in the corner they shared their dream the answer was immediate a no we don't lend to people like you we walked out of that building and our father went to the pub across the road he never recovered neither did we

---

33 june 2010

wrong shoes

shoes wrong shoes
why are you wearing
wrong shoes

who put them there
who said wear these
they pinch the toes
compress the soul
rub at the heels

shoes wrong shoes
why are you wearing
wrong shoes

take them off
let your feet out
hear them breathe
a sigh of hope
hope in the dirt
dust
depth
at home in the earth
wriggling presence
as a serpent signs the desert sands
wiradjuri connected
deep in creations genesis

spirit whispers
welcome back

no shoes
walk at one in this holy place[34]

---

34 june 2009

exile II

    i try to find my way back home
    there is no home

    i try to find my way back
    there is no way back

    i try to find my way
    there is no way

    i try to find my
    there is no me

    i try to find
    there is no thing to be found

    i tried
    i no longer try

    i
    i am in exile[35]

exile is the place beyond country beyond any evidence of belonging you are in exile when what you encompass on the outside is at odds with who you are on the inside and there is no way of bridging the chasm between when you are dispossessed of country and all that goes with it you are in exile on someone elses country where ever you are is not yours the country within does not communicate with the country you are standing upon no amount of effort to belong is sufficient until you come home even then the destruction of invasion and genocide has balanced the life source and you remain in exile even just a little bit

---

35 june 2009

known

being known
lying naked on the plains
open
free
vulnerable
shivering with each touch of sun
each whisper of breeze
exploring places
previously hidden
private
unknown
those covered by your own hands
embarrassed

yet you are warmed
in the awareness of being known
for the little you are
fragmented
whole
shimmering with life
blossoming
as wattle bursting into colour
transitioning the seasons
from slumber
at the dawn of spring

being known,
stands beckoning
midwife at the dawn of time[36]

being known is coming home it is that moment when you step on country and all around you seem to shout gawyanbanha when i went

---

36 june 2009

to the baarka recently i was met as i crossed into country by firstly an old man emu and his chicks followed by a wedgetail eagle and small mob of kangaroos it was as if they knew i was coming had come to welcome walking on the dirt sitting by the river watching the stars at dawn all scream you are home we know who you are looking at our possible lineage it has its beginning on those waters

where were you

    where were you yesterday
    yesterday your absence
    was visible
    vocal
    conspicuous

    where were you yesterday
    yesterday you stayed hidden
    no evidence to
    evoke
    any sense of hope

    yet...

    today you are here
    albeit small insignificant
    prolific buds of pink
    on harsh brittle brown limbs
    signs of life
    about to blossom
    springing from the shimmering skeleton
    its winter tomb

    calling to those
    who care to notice
    i am here
    yesterday
    today
    forever[37]

kin and country dance the seasons sometimes with great fanfare sometimes they just creep up on you as one demonstration of life and

---

37 june 2009

beauty is replaced seamlessly by another sometimes we are preoccupied with what is here now forgetting it will be replaced by another another and another we fail to see the signs and signals each give off not looking too busy disconnected from all we share country with slow down look listen hear and you will not be surprised by its arrival but a participant in that arrival

another australian soldier dies in afghanistan
– jane bardon reported this story on saturday 10 july 2010

i was present the day benny went to war
over there
i wasn't sure where over there was
or what we were fighting for
i doubt that benny knew either
yet they said go so go he did
saying little more than see ya mate
full of nervous energy like a grand final footballer
on the first saturday in september

benny was the scrawny kid in grade 3
i was new to the school he was my class buddy
sharing a lifetime of moments
we tackled growing up together
i laid awake at night imagining him
over there
dodging danger in the same irrepressible way
marking our progress by where we were
on the first saturday in september

got a couple of emails from him
from over there
never said much suppose he couldnt
except it was dusty and dirty
and the locals were unfriendly
reading between the lines
it was no church picnic
he hinted he couldnt wait to be home
sometime before the first saturday in september

i was there the day benny came home
from over there

birra-bina-birra...

the band played all solemn like
as the plane rolled to a halt
we all stood still lost in our memories
as the flag draped coffin was lowered down
and slow marched to the waiting hearse
somebody spoke of heroes and bravery and the anzac spirit
and bennys mum cried for all of us
sometime before the first saturday in september[38]

a simple ode to the futility of war nothing else to say

the roustabouts clout

he was a big man
knew his way around the ring
fought some big names
light heavy champion
in the navy so the rumours go
likes to throw his weight around
specially if he sensed a weakness
just a niggle and niggle
hoping for a fight

there wasn't much to the roustabout
small and wiry just a kid
good with his hands fast on his feet
had to be picking up fleeces
for a team of 200 a day shearers
he looked the typical patsy
an easy target
and so the game began

the lad said forget it
hes not worth it
the sheds nearly over
out of here in a couple of days
forget him
but a king hit in the tucker line
changed all that
the roustabout went down
but stood to call the big man outside

money changed hands
pragmatically placed on reputation and size
bare knuckle scrapping is not for the faint hearted
yet the choice of the roustabout
no gloves to soften the blows

gloves would slow his hands
his speed and agility his only hope
skipping ducking weaving
landing lightning fast punches
he led the big man a merry dance

when the dust settled
only one was standing
battered and bruised
and the lad walked away with the cash[39]

my father and his older brother were shearers from a very young age shearing in the early 1940s was a tough game for a kid of 14 often in sheds with much older men and little to do but smoke drink and fight my father told many a story of boxing matches some arranged some the result of an argument others alcohol fuelled he figured in most and this is one of those yarns he told us as kids

---

39 june 2010

song for a childhood lost

she was just a little girl innocence walking
never stopped talking open free
he was her father whom she trusted completely
yet the touch of his hand was more than she knew
and innocence slipped away
somewhere in the middle of the night
all alone in a place that was home
all alone homeless deserted

butterflies are free polar bears are too
yet she couldnt fly trapped in her cocoon
prematurely stunted no wings to be free

and the pain lingers on
far beyond the moment it all began
sun may shine roses may blown
the sound of children playing in the street
sounds like witches chattering
as the sunshine slips away
where did it go shouldnt she know
whether to hate withering anger
to destroy that which destroyed her
or is there another land
where the dark night of the lost
is dissipated by the morning rays of hope

butterflies are free polar bears are too
some day she will fly soaring in the sky
launched by her imagination innocent and free[40]

---

40 june 2010

this is an ode to a young person deeply betrayed by someone who should have loved her her bravery in telling her story and getting justice was and is an inspiration she is now a mother and wife and continues to blossom despite what may have crippled someone else

ya gotta limp a little

ya gotta limp a little
teeter totter
take a risk a little
roughen up the edges
smudge the ink
fade to black
now and then
nothings learnt
on a smooth road
only the potholes
allow colours to rise

ya gotta limp a little
to have anything to say
only when
youve scraped your knees
on the gravel road
can others see you bleed
bleeding makes you real
of interest to the world
prune in june
colour perfume in the spring

ya gotta limp a little
bend break cry a little
discover hidden hopefulness
courage and compassion
tears water the seeds
of character germinating
in the still-point of soul
buried securely
under the myths of
safety happiness blame
its a shame finding ways

> to avoid being cracked
> open by life
> so the light can get in
>
> ya gotta limp a little[41]

this was not written for the statement from the heart but captures the idea of makarrata walking with a limp after justice has been performed the statement from the heart promises us that there is a time after voice treaty truth where the light will get in and we as a nation will begin to walk differently to walk with a limp with the memory of a different time and the knowledge of being renewed of being reborn australia will be different and will be known by a different name

---

41 line attributed to tom waits july 2010

lost somewhere in between

fast takeaway
breezy sleazy breakaway
from responsible living

slim jim slopes
through the late night solitude
illuminated bleakly
by lazy streetlights
and cars cat like
cutting the silence in shards
before disappearing
in a hazy red glare
lost somewhere in between

slim jim holds on tight
to bundy bear
both rocking precariously
seeking some familiar landmark
finding none they zigzag
down the centre of the road
russian roulette in wobbly boots
on a journey to nowhere
another long night
in the promised land
unable or unwilling to deliver
on dreams it helped to birth

lost somewhere in between
hope and despair
cold comfort and
bottle shop doorways
unfriendly cops and
marauding teenagers
slim jim keeps on walking

in search of the
stories beginning
fearing how it
may all end
forever lost
somewhere in between[42]

will someone tell me what this is about

---

42 july 2010

i wasnt done walking[43]

just drop me back
where you picked me up
i wasn't done walking
going nowhere in particular
destination unplanned
unknown unwanted unnecessary
just gonna keep on walking
staying close enough to self
to see what's going down
far enough away not to care

just drop me back
where you picked me up
i wasn't done walking
walking is the destination
no need to arrive
achieve win or lose
just gonna keep on walking
living in the moment
touched by the sound
each footstep makes

just drop me back
where you picked me up
i wasn't done walking
no shortcuts to make
no rattling rail to jump
only an eye on the horizon
just gonna keep on walking
no need for friends
the call of the road
walks on forever

just drop me back
where you picked me up
i wasn't done walking

---

43 july 2010 line attributed to tom waits

sometimes we are too busy picking people up we don't let them take the journey that is theirs we want them to have what we have what makes us comfortable and secure first peoples are process people not people who look for outcomes results possessions it is all about walking walking country walking with country walking without the necessity to know where we are going where we are and what we are doing may seem of no value to do but for us it is all there is not arriving not possessing not producing is in fact arriving possessing producing in our own way

bulbil - feather

    feather (bubil)
    lying (dargim-birra) at my feet (warra)
    shuddering, (yirinya)
       shifting (waya)
    lifting (balabalamanha)
       floating (baalmanha)
    rising (barra-yawa-nha)
       exploring (nga-bin-gaa-nha)
    unseen (wirray-ngaa-mi-nya)
       unfelt (wirray-marra)
    whispers (birra-bina-birra) of air (bubu)

    negotiating the contours
    of my presence

    wandering (wagirra)
      back (bilin-nga-ya)
         forward (dayangun)
        up (nganha-duwalany)
          down (nganha-darrany)
    light (ngiriny)
      lively (girra-girra)
    silent (muguwar)
      out of sight (wayanmarra)
    returning home (ngulagambilhanha)

    on song lines of air
    beyond my senses

nothing else to say really

bila ngayirr
(the river is sacred)

> bila winhanga-y-gunha-nha balan-dha
> > the river remembers the beginning long ago
>
> bila dabu-ya-rra-murun yambuwan
> > the river gives life to everything
>
> bila marramarra nguram-bang
> > the river creates country (home)
>
> bila winhanga-garra-garra
> > the river knows everything
>
> bila wirray wang-nha
> > the river does not forget (or forgive)
>
> yindyamarra bila
> > respect the river
>
> bila yindyamarra-nhugu
> > (and) the river will respect you

circles

    maarung
    in the sky
    birrang-dha
    on the ground
    manhang-dhu
    in the veins beneath
    guwangayang-dha warraga (under there)

    circles
    maarung
    hold knowing
    marragarra gulbangidyilinya (knowing self)
    healing
    murungidyal
    being
    dhurinya

    circles
    maarung
    bring us all together
    ngungganha ngumbaaydyil
    speak
    yalbilinya (speak, learn)
    listen
    wudhagarbinya
    reflect
    winhangadurinya
    decide
    ngunggiyalarra (agree together)

    circles
    maarung
    educate
    yalmambirra (teach)

admonish
naabarra (reprimand)
repair
bagaraybang (restored)

circles
maarung
build-up
diraa-wamarra
breakdown
garruumarra
begin (ning)
gabingidyal
complete
wanhamarra

unseen
unheard
invisible

yes in a world of no

a prose poem in six stanzas
(with interludes from thomas merton)

introduction

lk 2:1-7

in those days a decree went out from emperor augustus that all the world should be registered this was the first registration and was taken while quirinius was governor of syria all went to their own towns to be registered. joseph also went from the town of nazareth in galilee to judea to the city of david called bethlehem because he was descended from the house and family of david he went to be registered with mary to whom he was engaged and who was expecting a child while they were there, the time came for her to deliver her child and she gave birth to her firstborn son and wrapped him in bands of cloth, and laid him in a manger because there was no place for them in the inn

    i

mary
    the mother of jesus
    a woman
    a person
    who said yes
    in a world of no

who said yes
    to giving life
    and breath
    to the son of god,
    the prince of peace

who said yes to god
in a world of no

in a world of no
>   peace
>   freedom
>   hope

in a world of no,
>   power
>   sovereignty
>   voice

in a world of no
>   recognition
>   visibility
>   safety

in a world of no
mary said yes
>   to birthing the
>   divine yes
>   bridging the abyss
>   between
>   the countries of
>   his father and
>   his mother

in a world of no
no place for
>   women
>   children
>   the unclean

in a world of no
mary said yes

(*pause*)

(*clapsticks*)

interlude

"christ our lord did not come to bring peace to the world as a kind of spiritual tranquilizer. he brought to his disciples a vocation and a task, to struggle in the world of violence to establish his peace not only in their own hearts but in society itself"[44]

(*clapsticks*)

(*pause*)

ii

no is the world's
default position of fear
fear of the transcendent
    of mystery
    of the unlike me
    of losing privilege to the privilege-less

no is obsessed with
maintaining
    power
    control
    othering

no is obsessed with
using violence in
    design
    words
    actions

no is obsessed with
holding to itself

---

44 merton, thomas, *the non violent alternative*, p. 13.

all that is
    privilege
    power
    resources
    people

no is obsessed with
    not seeing,
    reducing others
    to persona nullius
    not real persons

(*pause*)

(*clapsticks*)

interlude:

"the person can never be properly understood outside the framework of social relationships and obligations..."

(*clapsticks*)

(*pause*)

iii

no remains
    today
    now
    in this present breath

no remains
in the lived experience
of those subjugated by
    violence
    invasion

extermination
genocide

no remains
in our people's lived experience
of being
    reduced
    redacted
    redrawn
    as the less than
    the deficit
    the excuse

no spoke loudly in
    1770
    1778
    1824
    1901
    2007
    2017
and in the unnumbered statements and
asks from our people
acp - after cook and philip[45]

of being used
    as collateral in
    the power game of politics
    the oppositional binary
    of yes no
    winner loser

---

45 1770 – the discovery
    1778 – the invasion
    1824 – the war of extermination
    1901 – the Constitution
    2007 – Northern Territory Emergency Response
    2017 - Turnbull's rebuttal of the Statement from the Heart

of being
    incidental damage in an ask
    without political ideology

of seeking
    only justice
    for what should be ours
    recognition and a voice
    to be seen and included
    not as less than
    but same as
    not as someone
    to be fixed
    but as a people who are
    65,000 years
    at home on country

a people contemporary to all ages

(*pause*)

(*clapsticks*)

interlude

the person finds (their) reason for existence in the realm of truth, justice, love and liberty........

(*clapsticks*)

(*pause*)

iv

mary said yes
in a world of no
    she turned fear

   into hope
   through faith and trust

her not knowing
became the bridge
into a new dawn
instead of the relentless
monotony of another sunset
clouded with
  disappointment
  failed promises
  infantilisation

her not knowing
soared above what she
  knew
  lived
  recalled
in
  story
  song
  dance

in the colonial memory of
  dispossession
  displacement
  deprivation

offering no
  pathway of return
  to the circle of wholeness

the circle of
  country
  kin
  custodial belonging

of
> respect
> responsibility
> reciprocity

(*pause*)

(*clapsticks*)

interlude

"if the person is to function rationally as a member of society, (they) must meet others on the common ground of reason"

(*clapsticks*)

(*pause*)

v

mary's yes
can be your yes

the yes of accepting
the outstretched hand,
the dream of a renewed nation
birthed in conciliation
and truth
repairing the fractured nation
as the yes mary bore
repaired the relationship
between god and creation

the relationship between
the always was and always will be
and those who
> came

>dispersed
>settled
>>without seeing

(*pause*)

(*clapsticks*)

interlude

"common decisions and efforts must be oriented towards the common good"[46]

(*clapsticks*)

(*pause*)

vi

mary heard
the voice of the first morning
'let there be....'

the voice heard
mary's voice
and saw that she was good

into the world came
our voice
for the common good

can we hear echoes
of these voices in our time
to say yes, here i am ?

the alternative?

---

46 merton, thomas, *the non-violent alternative*, p. 52.

the judas kiss
thirty pieces of silver
for the souls of the first people

make mary's yes
your yes

(*clapsticks*)

garragiy[47]

---

47 yes it is

you are like dogs
mirrimirri-nhu
dog-like you

a prose poem for two voices
matthew 15:21-28

jesus left that place and went away to the district of tyre and sidon just then a canaanite woman from that region came out and started shouting, 'have mercy on me lord son of david my daughter is tormented by a demon' but he did not answer her at all and his disciples came and urged him, saying, 'send her away, for she keeps shouting after us' he answered 'i was sent only to the lost sheep of the house of israel' but she came and knelt before him saying 'lord help me' he answered 'it is not fair to take the children's food and throw it to the dogs' she said 'yes lord yet even the dogs eat the crumbs that fall from their masters table' then jesus answered her 'woman, great is your faith let it be done for you as you wish' and her daughter was healed instantly

this passage is a disturbing
uncomfortable
insight into
the embedded racism
within jesus' contemporary society

it was so embedded
jesus speaks it
in this social encounter
without reflection
or insight into
his spoken words

his mission was

selective
exclusive
based on
race and identity
not on inclusive love

'it is not fair to take the children's food and throw it to the dogs'

> *mirrimirri-nhu*
> *you are like dogs*

(*clap sticks – 3 times*)

raise your voice
say what needs to be said
don't be put off
by the righteous
and their privileged
blindness
the embedded certainty
that they are the chosen

> *mirrimirri-nhu*
> *you are like dogs*

(*clap sticks – 3 times*)

raise your voice
ask for what is yours
what you need
do not allow them
recourse to deafness
and ages old racism
the status quo
the way it is

> *mirrimirri-nhu*

> *you are like dogs*

(*clap sticks – 3 times*)

raise your voice
stand your ground
make your words heard
your meaning clear
your need is urgent
not to be rebuffed
ignored
belittled

> *mirrimirri-nhu*
> *you are like dogs*

(*clap sticks – 3 times*)

raise your voice
touch a nerve
unhinge the privilege
of a considered opinion
an accepted truism
buried in ideology
traditionally correct
for those it protects

> *mirrimirri-nhu*
> *you are like dogs*

(*clap sticks – 3 times*)

raise your voice
even the camp dogs
eat the unwanted scraps
the bits lying on the ground
left by those

who eat first
are we not
more than they

> *mirrimirri-nhu*
> *you are like dogs*

(*clap sticks – 3 times*)

raise your voice
make them hear
the sounds of ancestors
from time before they came here
crying for justice
witnessing genocide
know that you belong
here on country

> *wirray-nhu mirrimirri*
> *you are not dogs*

(*clap sticks – 3 times*)

raise your voice
make it known
convince the naysayers
receive what is yours
healing
wholeness
belonging
respect

> *wirray-nhu mirrimirri*
> *you are not dogs*

(*clap sticks – 3 times*)

raise your voice

for your little ones
for those yet to be
for those who have never left
healing comes
in a voice spoken
a listening heart
hope restored

(*clap sticks – 3 times*)

>   *mayiny-nhu*
>   *you are persons*

(*clap sticks – 3 times*)

raise your voice
this is the beginning
opening the way
repairing the fracture
in our personhood
our nationhood
our past
our future

(*clap sticks – 3 times*)

>   *mayiny-yanhinya*
>   *we are persons*

(*clap sticks – 3 times*)